# SCHIRMER'S LIBRARY
OF MUSICAL CLASSICS

JOSEPH HAYDN

Twenty Sonatas

For the Piano

Edited and Fingered by

LUDWIG KLEE and DR. SIGMUND LEBERT

Book I contains a Biographical Sketch of the Author by

DR. THEODORE BAKER

IN TWO BOOKS

Book I (Nos. 1-10) — Library Vol. 295

Book II (Nos. 11-20) — Library Vol. 296

G. SCHIRMER, Inc.

DISTRIBUTED BY

7777 W. BLEMOUND RD. P.O. BOX 13819 MILWAUKEE, WI 53213

JOSEPH HAYDN, the "creator of modern instrumental music" and "father of the symphony," was born on March 31, 1732, at the little village of Rohrau in lower Austria. At the age of six his education in music and the homelier branches was taken in charge by a relative named Frankh, a severe master and able teacher, under whom his precocious musical talent developed so rapidly that his singing attracted the notice of Reutter, the Kapellmeister of St. Stephens in Vienna, who engaged him as a chorister. Haydn's beautiful soprano retained Reutter's favor until his voice began to break; then, however, he was dismissed from the choir at the first opportunity. His thorough practical training in music now stood him in good stead, enabling him at first to earn a living by giving private lesssons; at the same time he kept up his practice on the violin and clavichord, and diligently studied the theory of composition; about this time (1751) he wrote his first mass. Becoming acquainted with Porpora, he accepted the situation of accompanist to the latter, receiving in return valuable instruction in Porpora's method of singing, though treated like a menial and performing menial service. But his chief recompense was the opportunity which he enjoyed of meeting distinguished musicians and patrons of art; his compositions, too, now found a certain vogue, especially the sonatas for clavier; and the first string-quartet was written (1755). On his appointment as director of the private orchestra of Count Morzin, with a salary of 200 florins, Haydn's prospects permitted of his getting married; his choice was a most unlucky one, his wife proving shrewish and in every way uncongenial. Still, judging from the serene and cheerful character of his music, Haydn's spirits were equal to the emergency. In 1759 he wrote his first symphony (in D-major), and a period of almost unrivaled productivity set in, hardly interrupted by the loss of his situation on the dissolution of the count's orchestra. In a few months (1761) he was made assistant Kapellmeister of Prince Esterhazy's band; though his patron died, his successor retained Haydn, who in 1769 became first Kapellmeister, a post which he held for 21 years, the band then being dissolved; but Prince Anton Esterhazy generously added 400 florins to the pension of 1,000 which his father had left to Haydn, so that the latter now possessed a modest competency, and removed to Vienna. In December, 1790, the impressario Salomon pursuaded Haydn to visit London, where they arrived on New Year's Day, 1791. Here Haydn "found himself the object of every species of attention; ambassadors and noblemen called on him, invitations poured in from all quarters, and he was surrounded by a circle of the most distinguished artists." His music was enthusiastically received, and Oxford conferred on him the degree of Doctor of Music. A second season in London had equally brilliant success. In June, 1792, he returned to Vienna, on the way passing through Bonn, where he met Beethoven, afterwards his pupil. A second journey to London in 1794 was the occasion of renewed ovations, and between the two musical seasons he spent the time at various country-seats of the English nobility. He journeyed homeward in August, 1795; during his absence a monument with his bust had been erected in his honor at his native village by his warm admirer, Count Harrach. Haydn's return had been hastened by Prince Nicolas Esterhazy, who re-engaged an orchestra, and required Haydn's active services as Kapellmeister. It was after this second visit to England tnat Haydn frequently remarked: "I did not become famous in Germany until I had been in England"--meaning probably that the English were the first to recognize his full deserts. The great composer, now at the zenith of his fame and creative power, wrote in the years immediately following his two grandest works, the "Creation" and the "Seasons," the words to both of which are translations of English poems (the former being combined from extracts from Milton's "Paradise Lost," the latter after Thomson's "Seasons"). After the beginning of the present century, however, Haydn's powers gradually waned; he died May 31 1809, in his house at Vienna.

Aside from the domestic affliction mentioned above, Haydn's life was remarkably free from the vicissitudes that so often beset great composers. His music reflects throughout the cheerful tranquillity and sportive humor of a spirit unvexed by irritating cares. The number of his works far exceeds 600, among them being 125 symphonies (or 191 if we count as such his 66 Divertissements, Sextets, etc.), 77 string-quartets, 35 trios for clavier, violin, and 'cello, 20 concertos for clavier, 175 pieces for barytone (this being the favorite instrument of Prince Paul Anton Esterhazy), and, besides the two great oratorios, numerous masses, Te Deums, offertories, etc. Among the first of his works published by Artaria of Vienna were 6 clavier sonatas, op. 30. In the history of music he occupies a foremost place on account of his development of the forms of the quartet and symphony, and of the resources of the orchestra in a modern sense—that of the individualization of the several instruments. "One of his most marked characteristics was his constant aim at perfection in his art. He once said, regretfully, to Kalkbrenner, 'I have only just learned in my old age how to use the wind-instruments, and now that I do understand them I must leave the world.' And to Griesinger he said that he had by no means come to the end of his powers; that ideas were often floating in his mind, by which he could have carried the art far beyond anything it had yet attained, had his physical powers been equal to the task."

TH. BAKER

Index.

Vol. I.

1. Allegro.  Page 3.

2. Presto.  Page 19.

3. Allegro.  Page 28.

4. Moderato.  Page 42.

5. Allegro con brio.  Page 50.

6. Moderato.  Page 61.

7. Allegro con brio.  Page 68.

8. Allegro moderato.  Page 76.

9. Moderato.  Page 90.

10. Allegretto innocente.  Page 102.

Index.

Vol. I.

Allegro.

1.  Page 3.

Presto.

2.  Page 19.

Allegro.

3.  Page 28.

Moderato.

4.  Page 42.

Allegro con brio.

5.  Page 50.

Moderato.

6.  Page 61.

Allegro con brio.

7.  Page 68.

Allegro moderato.

8.  Page 76.

Moderato.

9.  Page 90.

Allegretto innocente.

10.  Page 102.

SONATA.

Abbreviations: *) M. T. signifies Main Theme; Ep., Episode; S. T., Sub-Theme; Cl. T., Closing Theme; D. G., Development-group; Md. T., Mid-Theme; R., Return; Tr., Transition; Cod., Codetta; I, II, III signify 1st, 2nd, and 3rd parts of a movement in song-form (Liedform).

JOSEPH HAYDN.

*) German equivalents: M. T. signifies Hauptsatz; Ep., Zwischensatz; S. T., Seitensatz; Cl. T., Schlusssatz; D. G., Durchführungssatz; Md.T., Mittelsatz; R., Rückgang; Tr., Übergang; Cod., Anhang; I. II. III., 1., 2. u. 3. Theil eines liedförmigen Satzes.

a) All arpeggios in this movement, when written unjoined for both hands, are to be begun and ended with both hands together.

Printed in the U. S. A.

11695

4

*) In such a rapid movement as this, trilled notes are executed in the manner indicated here.

11695

a) In this chord, strike all the tones in succession, from the lowest to the highest, the highest tone receiving the greatest stress.

10 Adagio. (♪ .= 80.)

a) In all arpeggios in which the wavy line ⸠ continues unbroken through both staves, the tones are to be struck in succession from the lowest to the highest, particular stress being given to the highest tone.

b) Here the hands commence together.

c) Like b).

11695

a) The grace-note G must be struck together with the A♯, F♯ entering immediately afterward.

a) The first of these grace-notes must be struck simultaneously with the accompaniment-note E.

Finale.

Presto. ($\downarrow$ = 84.)

a) A considerable pause should be made after the hold itself.   b) Here a brief pause only.

Adagio.

a) Continue after a brief pause.

b) A prolonged pause here.

a) As on Page 14 a).   b) As on Page 14 b).   c) Trill without after-beat, but ending on the principal note.

SONATA.

Abbreviations: M. T., signifies Main Theme; Ep., Episode; S. T., Sub-Theme; Cl. T., Closing Theme; D. G., Development-group; Md. T., Mid-Theme; R., Return; Tr. Transition; Cod., Codetta; I, II, and III, 1st, 2nd, and 3rd parts of a movement in song-form (Lied-form.)

JOSEPH HAYDN.

Printed in the U. S. A.

a) After the hold a considerable pause should be made.

a) After the hold, a brief pause should be made.

a) Duly subordinate the accompaniment.

b) In rapid tempo, the turn between two notes of this value may best be executed as follows:

a) After the hold, make a brief pause.

a) Continue after a short pause.

SONATA.

Abbreviations: M. T. signifies Main Theme; Ep., Episode; S. T., Sub-Theme; Cl. T., Closing Theme; D. G., Development-group; Md. T., Mid-Theme; R., Return; Tr., Transition; Cod., Codetta; I, II, and III, signify 1st, 2nd, and 3rd parts of a movement in song-form (Lied-form).

JOSEPH HAYDN.

a) Make a considerable pause after the hold itself.

b) This accompaniment-figure in the left hand must be subordinated to the right-hand part throughout

11697

Printed in the U S. A.

c) Both hands must begin and end the *arpeggio* together, and with a *crescendo* in the right-hand part, so that its highest tone may be the most prominent.

a) As at b) on 1st Page of this Sonata.

b) Begin the embellishment together with the first bass note.

a) After lifting both hands, proceed instantly.
b) Make a considerable pause after this hold.

a) As at b), on 1st page of this Sonata.

a) As at c), on Page 29.

Adagio cantabile. ($\quad$ = 50)

a) Throughout the movement the melody must be made duly prominent, but without any harshness.

b) The execution of these 2 measures is like that of the first 2. In all cases, embellishments take their time-value from that of the principal note with which they are connected by a slur, as the above example shows.

a) This grace is also played as a short turn in 4 equal notes, falling on the sixth 16th-note of the accompaniment-figure.
b) The 3 grace-notes coincide, as a triplet, with the third 16th-note of the accompaniment-figure.

Finale.

Tempo di Menuetto. ($\bullet$ = 126.)

*) The time-value of this grace is taken from that of the preceding eighth-rest, as follows:

a)

SONATA.

Abbreviations: M.T. signifies Main Theme; Ep., Episode; S.T., Sub-Theme; Cl.T., Closing-Theme; Cod., Codetta; Tr., Transition; D.G., Development Group; I, II, III, 1st, 2nd, and 3rd parts of a movement in song-form (Liedform.)

Revised and Fingered by
LUDWIG KLEE.

JOSEPH HAYDN.

Printed in the U.S.A.

SONATA.

Abbreviations: M. T. signifies Main Theme; Ep., Episode; S. T., Sub-Theme; Cl. T., Closing Theme; D. G., Development-group; Md. T., Mid-Theme; R., Return; Tr., Transition; Cod., Codetta; I, II, III, signify 1st, 2nd, and 3rd parts of a movement in song-form (Liedform.)

Allegro con brio. (♩ = 96.)

JOSEPH HAYDN.

a) The short turn in small notes is intended for inexpert players. In the original, these turns are all marked thus:

Printed in the U. S. A.

a) easier: b) After the hold a fairly long pause should be made.

a) Adagio.

a) Sustain the hold, and then proceed without interruption.

Tempo I.

poco rit. *a tempo.* M.T.

a) This hold is longer than the preceding one; before continuing, a fairly long pause should be made.
11699

a) Inexpert players may omit the first note of each turn, as before.
b) The hold sustained, and followed by a brief pause.

11699

a) Duly subordinate the accompaniment. b) ♪♪♪♪♪♪♪♪ easier: ♪♪♪♪♪♪♪

c) Strike all the tones of the chord in succession, from the lowest to the highest, and connect the preceding b with the high c.

Finale.

Allegro. (♩. = 63.)

SONATA.

Abbreviations: M.T. signifies Main Theme; Ep., Episode; S.T., Sub-Theme; Cl.T., Closing Theme; D.G., Development-Group; Md.T., Mid-Theme; R., Return; Tr., Transition; Cod., Codetta; I, II, III, signify 1st, 2nd, and 3rd parts of a movement in song-form (Liedform.)

JOSEPH HAYDN.

*) In this motive the sign ∾ does not signify a turn with the ordinary division ▤▤▤, but serves as an abbreviation for the figure: ▤▤▤ which, in analogy with the initial motive, must be imitated throughout the movement in all similar situations.

11700

11700

Scherzando.

Allegro con brio. (♩ = 120.)

Menuetto.
Moderato. (♩ = 132.)

a) ♪ 	b) Commence with the principal note, as at a).	c) As above.

SONATA.

Abbreviations: M.T. signifies Main Theme; Ep., Episode; S.T., Sub-Theme; Cl.T., Closing Theme; D.G., Development-group; Md.T., Mid Theme; R., Return; Tr., Transition; Cod., Codetta; I and II, 1st and 2nd parts of a movement in song-form (Liedform.)

Allegro con brio. (♩ = 138.)

JOSEPH HAYDN.

*) In view of the rapid tempo, only an inverted mordent, consisting of 3 equal notes, accenting the first, can well be played:

Printed in the U.S.A.

a) easier

a) Strike the tones in succession, from the lowest to the highest, and hold all down.

b) As above.

11701

Finale.

Presto, ma non troppo.(♩ = 144.)

a) This accompaniment-figure must be kept duly subordinate to the melody.　b) easier

SONATA.

Abbreviations: M.T. signifies Main Theme; Ep., Episode; S.T., Sub-Theme; Cl.T., Closing Theme; D.G., Development-group; Md.T., Mid-Theme; R., Return; Tr., Transition; Cod., Codetta.

Allegro moderato. (= 80.)

JOSEPH HAYDN.

a) In this style of accompaniment the left hand must always be subordinated to the right, here playing *mf* instead of *f* and so on in like proportion.

b)

Printed in the U.S.A.

a) Sustain holds for about the value of 4 quarter-notes.   b)   c)

poco rit.

11702

a) This repetition of the principal theme should be rendered somewhat prominent.

b)  c)  etc. d) Execute this and the following trill as shown above at c).

e) Subordinate this accompaniment slightly, in contrast to the two principal parts.

f) Play these tones in succession from the lowest up to the highest, with a crescendo combined with a poco ritardando.

11702

a) As at a), preceding page.
c) As at e), preceding page.

poco rit.

11702

a) Proceed, without an intervening pause, from the first hold to the second, and prolong this latter to a time-value about double that of the actual note-value, thus:

Finale.

Presto. (♩ = 132.)

a) The following mode of execution will suffice for inexpert players:

11702

SONATA.

Abbreviations: M. T., signifies Main Theme; Ep., Episode; S. T., Sub-Theme, Cl. T., Closing Theme; D. G., Development-group; Md. T., Mid-Theme, R., Return; Tr., Transition; Cod., Codetta; I, II, and III., 1st, 2nd, and 3rd parts of a movement in song-form. (Liedform.)

JOSEPH HAYDN.

a) Here an inverted turn, as we have written out above, would appear more tasteful.

b) This style of accompaniment ought always to be kept comparatively subordinate.

c) [music example]   d) Begin and close the arpeggio with both hands together.

11703

a) b) c) As at b) preceding page. d) As at b).

11703

91

a) The accompaniment (and also when it lies in the right-hand part itself) must, in what follows, always be comparatively subordinate to the melody.

a) easier: b) c) As at a) on page 96.

Finale.
Allegro assai. (♩ = 144.)

a) These holds should be so sustained that the notes affected by them occupy about double the time which their actual value demands:

11703

*) Execution as above.

11703

SONATA.

Abbreviations: M. T. signifies Main Theme; Ep., Episode; S. T., Sub-Theme; Cl. T., Closing Theme; D. G., Development-Group; Md. T., Mid-Theme; R., Return; Tr., Transition; Cod., Codetta; I, II, and III, 1st, 2nd, and 3rd parts of a movement in song-form (Liedform.)

JOSEPH HAYDN.

Allegretto innocente. ($\bullet$ = 72.)

10.

a) 𝄞 easier: 𝄞 b) 𝄞 easier: 𝄞 c) After the hold lift both hands together, and continue after a brief pause. d) 𝄞 easier: 𝄞

Printed in the U.S.A.

Var. M.T.

a) As at c) on preceding page.

11704

a) Sustain long, and proceed only after a prolonged pause: b) easier: